Fawns

by Anne Wendorff

BELLWETHER MEDIA • MINNEAPOLIS, MN

Note to Librarians, Teachers, and Parents:

Blastoff! Readers are carefully developed by literacy experts and combine standards-based content with developmentally appropriate text.

Level 1 provides the most support through repetition of high-frequency words, light text, predictable sentence patterns, and strong visual support.

Level 2 offers early readers a bit more challenge through varied simple sentences, increased text load, and less repetition of high-frequency words.

Level 3 advances early-fluent readers toward fluency through increased text and concept load, less reliance on visuals, longer sentences, and more literary language.

Level 4 builds reading stamina by providing more text per page, increased use of punctuation, greater variation in sentence patterns, and increasingly challenging vocabulary.

Level 5 encourages children to move from "learning to read" to "reading to learn" by providing even more text, varied writing styles, and less familiar topics.

Whichever book is right for your reader, Blastoff! Readers are the perfect books to build confidence and encourage a love of reading that will last a lifetime!

This edition first published in 2009 by Bellwether Media, Inc.

No part of this publication may be reproduced in whole or in part without written permission of the publisher. For information regarding permission, write to Bellwether Media, Inc., Attention: Permissions Department, Post Office Box 19349, Minneapolis, MN 55419.

Library of Congress Cataloging-in-Publication Data
Wendorff, Anne.
    Fawns / by Anne Wendorff.
        p. cm. – (Blastoff! readers. Watch animals grow)
    Includes bibliographical references and index.
    Summary: "A basic introduction to fawns. Developed by literacy experts with simple text and full color photography for students in kindergarten through third grade"–Provided by publisher.
    ISBN-13: 978-1-60014-240-6 (hardcover : alk. paper)
    ISBN-10: 1-60014-240-0 (hardcover : alk. paper)
    1. Fawns–Juvenile literature. I. Title.

QL737.U55W436 2009
599.65'139–dc22
                                    2008033537

Contents

A mother deer
has fawns.
A mother deer
is called a **doe**.

A newborn fawn is weak and **wobbly**. It must learn to stand and walk.

A fawn grows strong in one week. Then it can walk with its mother.

Fawns are born
with four teeth.
They drink
milk from
their mother.

Fawns grow more
teeth to eat
solid food.
Their favorite
foods are berries,
grass, and nuts.

Fawns are born with light brown **fur**. They have white spots on their back.

The spots fade
as a fawn grows.
The spots are
gone by winter.

Fawns love to
play. They run,
kick, and leap.

Male fawns will grow into big, strong **bucks**. Bucks grow big **antlers**.

Glossary

antlers—bony horns on the heads of male deer

buck—a male deer

doe—a female deer

fur—the hair covering an animal

wobbly—shaky or unsteady

To Learn More

AT THE LIBRARY

Cooper, Jason. *Fawn to Deer*. Vero Beach, Fla.: Rourke, 2003.

Jaffe, Elizabeth Dana. *Deer Have Fawns*. Minneapolis, Minn.: Compass Point Books, 2002.

Ryder, Joanne. *A Fawn in the Grass*. New York: Henry Holt and Company, 2001.

ON THE WEB

Learning more about fawns is as easy as 1, 2, 3.

1. Go to www.factsurfer.com.

2. Enter "fawns" into the search box.

3. Click the "Surf" button and you will see a list of related Web sites.

With factsurfer.com, finding more information is just a click away.

Index

The images in this book are reproduced through the courtesy of: Bruce MacQueen, front cover; Cynthia Kidwell, p. 5; Derris Lanier, p. 7; St. Nick, p. 9; Tatiana Grozetskaya, p. 11; Floris Slooff, p. 13; Mira / Alamy, p. 15; Skip Brown / Getty Images, p. 17; Jack Milchanowski, p. 19; Nathan Hager, p. 21.